DANIEL OWENS

The Manual
for
SOUL
FISHING

The Vision

"Follow me and I will make you a fisherman of men."

Matthew 4:19

I heard God's quiet, still voice. Why was God telling me this? I have been following Him a long time. People often ask if God still speaks to His people today? Absolutely! I will answer that with a resounding yes. There is no physical place I have to be in to hear God's voice. I can be in my car, in my bed, or even in the shower. Sometimes even when my spirit is in a low place, God speaks words of love and encouragement.

On April 16, 2019 I was sitting on a plane far from home. I was thanking God for allowing me to be the vessel used to preach salvation to so many people in India. As I was reflecting on all that had happened there, God spoke the words from Matthew 4:18-20 to me. I began to pray and seek Him right there on the plane. I soon came to realize that He wanted me to show others how to actively search for lost souls. It was no longer enough for me to win souls, but He wanted me to share with others His formula. God uses His people to do His fishing.

God showed me myself in a vision writing a manual on fishing for souls. Sitting on that plane, I was convinced beyond a shadow of a doubt that God was giving me an urgent assignment. The press was such that I knew the manual had to be published in the same year that God gave me the vision. As you read it, read it with an open mind and an open spirit as we explore being fishers of men.

In this manual I want the readers to learn the techniques of fishing, the when, what, how, and where. In 2019 there are many empty seats in our churches. Why? We as Christians, have been trying to fill up our churches with people from other churches and not with the lost souls in the world. After reading this manual, I want you to be able to grow church membership, Bible Study attendance, and I want your very life to be transformed.

Chapter 1: Fishing Obstacles

Fishing takes plenty of supernatural patience. You have to wait and wait for something (someone) to bite your bait. In the natural most people we know fish for sport; while others fish to feed their families and make a living. In the scripture Simon Peter and Andrew made their living from fishing. Yet Jesus told them to forget all of that and come follow Him. This was not a small thing Jesus was asking them. There was no mention of being paid a salary. But still they left their nets and immediately followed Him regardless of the circumstances. (John 1:40-42, Matthew 4:18-20)

Jesus taught by using parables using the day to day things that his listeners were familiar with! The two brothers in the scripture understood fishing so Jesus spoke to them about being fishers of men.

We can become fishers of men without going very far. It doesn't have to be deep in the ocean or across the sea. We will find fish "in our own back yards". Sometimes the "pier" is right outside your door. Most of the time when we fish for souls it won't be behind a pulpit. God has commanded and is commanding that we make it a part of our daily living.

Don't get discouraged if you find yourself fishing in a familiar place and the fish do not receive you because they "know" you. Jesus also had this problem. "Truly I say to you, no prophet is acceptable in his hometown" (Luke 4:24) What we can be assured of that the seed we plant, someone else will water and God will get the glory for the increase. Often it will take going beyond our neighborhoods to catch fresh fish.

Fishing has always been a part of my life. When I was young, I remember my father and I spending time together fishing. He taught me what he knew about fishing. At the time I was thinking, "All I have to do is throw this rod in the water with a worm on the hook and bingo, I catch a fish." Not so! It takes a special technique. If it's true in the natural, it's also true in the spiritual realm. A person who knows how to fish can teach others to fish.

Our young people today are not as nature conscious as their parents or grandparents were. A lot of them have interest in indoor activities such as Fortnite. Because many of us are clueless concerning these games, we fail to reach this generation because we don't know what our common ground is. Yet we have to find the "parable" that will reach them and teach them. There is a

Chinese proverb: "Give a man a fish, and you feed him for a day. Teach a man to fish and you feed him for a lifetime."

We continue to preach to people who are already saved. We, as the Body of Christ, have not put in the work to fish for souls. There are so many "fish" waiting to be caught, but we have to put in the work. The assignment is for every believer- not just for the Apostle, Prophet, Evangelist, Pastor, or Teacher. The Bible says that the harvest truly is plenteous, but the laborers are few; Pray ye therefore the Lord of the harvest, that He will send forth laborers into His harvest. (Matthew 9:37-38) What does this mean? There is a lot of ripe fruit out there to pick, but the laborers to do it are very few. God has already set the pace. He has allowed the fruit to flourish and ripen, but the laborers are not in place. Many times in the spring we find ourselves excited because watermelon, peaches, strawberries, and other fruit are ready to pick and eat. But the hardest work to do is collect all of the fruit that has ripened. So it is with fishing. There are many people out there that God has prepared. He has set the pace for them to receive His word and accept salvation. He only needs ordinary people who believe to share the good news of the gospel with them.

Overpopulation

According to Sanco Industries fish overpopulation is almost guaranteed in private ponds and lakes that are rarely fished in.

Understanding this in the natural helps us grasp it in the spiritual. There are a lot of places in the world that are overpopulated with fish. Sanco Industries goes on to tell what happens when you have an overpopulation of fish. "Fish will start fighting over food source and many fish may become stunted and many will die." That sounds like a lot of our communities in the United States and around the world. Many people are fighting and killing over possessions because they are in an overpopulated area.

A Habitat ceases to be a habitat when it becomes polluted from overpopulation. Fish become uncomfortable in their natural habitats. When they die, the water becomes polluted which causes more deaths. That is why it is so important to fish daily and put fish in the boat. We need to make the water, which is the world, a better place.

The Apostle Paul told his mentee, Timothy to do the work of an evangelist. How does that relate to us today? We are to go out and evangelize. That is to simply share the good news of the gospel. This can be done in a grocery store, at school, at a track meet, a football game, etc. As we go about our daily lives, the Holy Spirit will bring people before you that desperately need to hear the good news of the gospel of Jesus Christ. We are to be beacons of light for Jesus Christ shining in the midst of darkness. Jesus said, "Let your light so shine before men, that they may see your good works and glorify your Father which is in Heaven". (Matthew 5:16-17) In other words, there should be something about us that people in darkness are curious about.

In my research about fishing I read about flash or light fishing where you shine the light on the water. When you fish in the darkness, the fish come up to see what is going on. When the fish come to the surface, they are caught with a net. When we shine our lights on places and situations and people that are in darkness, they can see Jesus through us. They will be able to move toward the light which is a life in Christ Jesus. As we teach them to fish, they will also do the work that God is calling for in such a time as this. Just as there are rewards that come from fishing, there are also rewards that will come from fishing for souls.

Chapter 2: Where do I Fish?

After Jesus was crucified and rose from the dead, He gathered His disciples together and gave them the great commission: "Go ye into all the world and preach the gospel to every creature. He that believeth and is baptized shall be saved, but he that believeth not shall be damned." (Mark 16:15-16)

All of us will not go all over the world to witness. But all of us are called to witness and it is important to know where and when you are assigned to witness. It may be to someone on your job, while working on a school project, in a Sunday School class. Just ask God to lead you as you become more comfortable with fishing.

With that being said, He gives us many, many places to fish. As I mentioned before, my Dad and I spent a lot of time fishing. My Dad referred to one of his favorite fishing spots as a honey hole. It was guaranteed that there would be many bites throughout the day. He knew that when we left we would have a cooler full of fish.

So to compare that with our spiritual walk as we become fishers of men, we have to find a place to fish in. There are things to consider when looking for a place to fish. A church full of disciples who are already clean and heading in the right direction is not a place to fish. We, as a people, have to go seek the lost-- those who have no church home, those who do not know Jesus as a personal savior. We need to go to the remote ponds, lakes, and seas where no one has considered fishing. This is where the biggest fish will be caught because the water has not been troubled. When fishing for souls keep in mind that the people you minister to might not always look like you or smell like you –you will encounter people that you've never communicated with.

Another consideration is the attitude that we fish with. Our daily prayer should be like David's "Create in me a clean heart, oh God and renew a right spirit within me". (Psalm 51:10) We need a willing spirit that recognizes that we may have to go beyond our comfort zone. In the natural, some of the best fish have been caught in places that were uncomfortable—places where it wasn't unusual to see mosquitoes and snakes. Just recently I was led to go preach the gospel in a place where there was no decent running water. The food was a far cry from what I was used to. But I had to take on the attitude of the Apostle Paul who realized that to reach people he could not be arrogant and think too highly of himself. When ministering to people, we have to be set apart yet not stick out like a sore thumb. Some of you might say, "Daniel, what do you mean by that?" You have to keep your agenda in mind. My mission was to preach the gospel to the lost. I wanted to be down to earth and reachable to them, yet not fall into sin myself.

We have to have a loving attitude when fishing. Those who have never known the love of Jesus have to see it reflected in us. Sometimes, especially when we are out of our comfort zone (compare this to walking through the bushes, being bitten by mosquitoes, looking for snakes trying to get to the perfect fishing spot), we may feel frustrated and unless we allow the Holy Spirit to renew us, that frustration may be visible to the souls we are trying to reach. No one wants to hear what a mean-spirited person is saying about the gospel.

So as you go out with a willing and loving spirit looking for a fishing spot there are four things to consider:

1. Do your homework first. Don't just show up at a place with a "Here I am" mentality and look for great results. You have to go in knowing something about the place you are going. When I was in India I knew that I was going to a village with a population of 3,000 that had no life- giving church.

2. Scope out the place. What is it infected with? How can I bring light to the dark areas? The day before I preached in India, the team visited the village to learn

something about it and the people who resided there. I knew that if I went in and immediately started talking about Jesus Christ, mental walls would go up. So I asked about families and customs, what types of foods do you enjoy, etc. Gathering information helps you to be more effective.

    3.   Hone in on the features of the community. For me I had to find out more about the community in India.

    4.   Be prayerful in looking for a place. God will begin to draw you to where He wants you to go and will start preparing the people to receive you. This is why God sent me to India to fish. The Bible tells us that the steps of a good man are ordered by the Lord. A good prayer to pray every day is similar to this one: "Lord, use me however you may want to during this day. Let me seize every opportunity to share Christ. Let me walk in love everyday that Your name will get the glory as I fish for souls. Lord, give me the opportunity for Your people to be drawn to You through me. Amen."

John 21 gives us the amazing testimony of how Jesus's disciples were rewarded for fishing exactly where He told them to cast their nets.

After these things Jesus shewed himself again to the disciples at the sea of Tiberias; and on this wise shewed he *himself.*

2 There were together Simon Peter, and Thomas called Didymus, and Nathanael of Cana in Galilee, and the *sons* of Zebedee, and two other of his disciples.

3 Simon Peter saith unto them, I go a fishing. They say unto him, We also go with thee. They went forth, and entered into a ship immediately; and that night they caught nothing.

4 But when the morning was now come, Jesus stood on the shore: but the disciples knew not that it was Jesus.

5 Then Jesus saith unto them, Children, have ye any meat? They answered him, No.

6 And he said unto them, Cast the net on the right side of the ship, and ye shall find. They cast therefore, and now they were not able to draw it for the multitude of fishes.

Keep in mind that these were professional fishermen. They knew practically everything there was to know about fishing. They knew where the honey spots were. They knew what the best time of day was to fish. But in this passage of scripture they had toiled all night without so much as a bite. Then here comes this stranger (for they didn't realize it was the resurrected Christ) telling them to cast their net on the right side. Jesus knew the longitude and the latitude for catching a multitude of fishes. Notice He didn't just lead them to a certain place in the sea but also gave them very specific instructions. Cast the net on the **right** side.

This is also how it is to be fishers of men. When you pray, fast, and allow God to lead you, He will show you His will and give you the answers you need to catch fish.

Chapter 3: Techniques of Fishing

There are seven fishing techniques on Fishing.com, and I want to talk about five of those techniques because this is very important. We don't want to use the wrong type of bait for the place we are fishing. Whether in the natural or in the spiritual realm you can fish all day and not get a bite if you are using the wrong bait for that habitat. We have to be cognizant of the habitat we are in. For example you can't fish for saltwater fish in a pond. There are different techniques you can use while fishing that can also be applied to fishing for souls.

The first technique I want to tell you about is **hand gathering**. Hand gathering needs no equipment, you actually use your bare hands. It includes trout tickling, pearl diving, noodling and flounder tramping. The fish are gathered with your hands. These fish don't go far into the ocean or deep in the pond. They can stay close to the shore because you have certain fish that can find their way under the ground in the water. Catfish can also be caught with hand gathering. When hand gathering you get in the water and feel around for the fish. Then you carefully bring it out with your hands.

This type of fishing in the spiritual realm is for those who grew up in church but left the ark of safety. They may have been church hurt or lost their connection with God. They are aware of who God is and are aware of His capabilities, but they have lost trust in Him. These souls want to be hidden in the water because they do not want to be found. They want to be overlooked because they do not want to go back to a place that has wounded them. So they find themselves hiding in the water. They sit at the bottom of their habitat and the food basically comes to them. They are not particular about what they eat; they will eat anything. They don't want to lose their position because they have convinced themselves that they feel just fine where they are. These fish know their habitat very well and they know the best place to hide. So as a soul fisher, this technique of hand gathering has to be done very carefully. These souls are the ones who have backslidden. As I said, they once knew Christ, but they left either because of circumstances, a mishap, or something or someone caused them to get disconnected from Christ. These particular fish such as trout or a pearl or flounder are actually big fish. These fish are some of the biggest fish you can ever think of because they know what to do to survive. As a backslider finds himself back in the water, he knows how to survive because he has lived there before and is very aware of his surroundings. So with hand gathering the biggest equipment you need is <u>patience</u> and a caring spirit to reach the soul. With hand gathering you cannot be rough because the fishes know what you are doing; they know you are coming for them. You have to be very gentle with this fish because they have been wounded. Many people who have left the church need this kind of fishing because nothing else will work. Hand gathering includes that friend you grew up in church with. You attended Sunday School together. There came a point in life where your paths went in different directions. Maybe during the college years this friend strayed away from the church. In order for this type of fishing to be effective you have to be close to the soul. <u>You have to be able to understand them and the situation they are in</u> <u>keeping in mind that they</u> <u>also know you</u>. I can't stress enough that you have to be very gentle and patient and show a lot of love. This technique may take more time, but keep in mind that when you catch this soul it is a big catch.

Paul writes to one of the churches that had backslidden in Galatians 3:1.

"You foolish Galatians! Who has bewitched you? Before your very eyes Jesus Christ was clearly portrayed as crucified." (NIV)

The second technique is **spear fishing**. This type of fishing can be done from the pier or on land, but most commonly is done by diving. Fishermen have historically used sharpened sticks and hand-held tools to pierce the fish. You have to be very precise when spear fishing, and it also takes a lot of patience. You see the fish floating or sailing through the water and you need to be ready to use your spear at the right time with the right speed and accuracy. So what in the world is spiritual spear fishing? Spiritual spear fishing is using things that shock such as a tragedy or a transformation in someone's life. These life changing events are used to spear souls. You're looking for that one particular soul that is out there alone...not around anyone else. When tragic things happen, people tend to want to turn to something greater than themselves, which we know is Jesus Christ. God will position you and give you the opportunity to share the good news while they are still in shock...while they are in a state of disbelief, a state of wondering how did I get to this point? Spear fishing is when God has allowed something to happen in their lives. Now God is going to use you to catch that one. When you spear fish in the natural, you don't necessarily have to be close to the fish. But you do need to study it as it floats and see where it is going. This can be compared to someone you are cordial with and perhaps you know her husband has died. You begin to make conversation with this person because chances are she needs someone to talk to. As this person begins to share with you, this is the perfect opportunity to ask, "Have you tried Jesus Christ?" With spear fishing, you grab the fish while they are still in shock.

Do you recall the story of Jairus's daughter? (Mark 5) Jairus's daughter was sick and died. Jesus came to the house and there were mourners there. Jesus put them out of the room because He was about to do a miracle and there was too much unbelief in the room. Jesus brought the little girl back to life. Can you imagine the look on the faces of those mourners when the little girl walked out of the room? Jesus performed a miracle and transformed lives. Many began to follow Him because of that. Jesus used spear fishing to draw them in. While they were still in shock, He caught them.

Netting technique is the third technique. Nets are meshes formed by knotting a thin thread used to trap fish, thus it is used by anglers who are attempting to catch large schools of fish. You can not fish with nets on the shore of any water. When you fish with net you have to push out, you have to go out into the deep water because the fishes on the shore do not go into the deep water. They do not know how to survive out there. But the ones who are in the deep water, such as the crabs, live there. It is their habitat. Let me note that you are looking for anything that lives under the water, so you're looking for more than fish. You're looking for crabs, oysters, scallops, and clams. I think sometimes we forget about them and just look for particular kinds of fish. So just keep in mind that with netting you want to go farther.

Fish travel in a community called a school. This is when you want to use a net. You want to grab as many fish and living things as possible with this net. This net is thrown out and goes down at a fast, rapid pace and traps the fish inside.

When fishing for souls, these are your mission trips where you minister to people who did not grow up in church; they are lost. Sometimes it means going to poverty- stricken areas where people have lost hope. It means going out to minister to teenagers. When netting, you want to go out and set up some time of outreach and simply show the love of Jesus Christ.

When fishing with a net you don't need a certain type of bait. All you need to do is be in the area. Just show up with love. An example of net fishing is my trip to India that I mentioned in an earlier chapter. Three hundred and fifty- four people accepted Jesus Christ in that village. That was a massive gain for the kingdom of God in a short time. A biblical example of net fishing is when Jesus fed 5,000 men by using a young boy's lunch which was two fish and five loaves of bread. They saw Jesus at work as He performed a miracle and gave them physical food as well as spiritual food. (John 6:1-14)

The fourth technique is **angling**. Angling is the most popular and most traditional method of fishing. Angling involves using a fishing rod and a hook. You are fishing for one fish at a time and you choose bait according to the type of fish you want to catch. Not all fish will be attracted to the same bait.

Spiritual angling starts with a conversation that draws a person in. You can be in line at a grocery store and strike up a conversation about football, basketball, or any type of sport. You might discover something you have in common. The right remark can lead to a conversation about Jesus. Your witness to them can draw them in. Angling is used when you are out and about just being friendly to people.

Nicodemus was a Pharisee, a religious ruler of the Jews who had heard about Jesus. He did not want to be seen talking to Jesus, so he went to him at night. Jesus had a conversation with Nicodemus telling him that he must be born again. Nicodemus was religious, but he had no concept of what it meant to know God. (John 3:1-21)

The fifth technique is **trapping.** Traps can have the form of a fishing weir or a lobster trap. This type of fishing involves luring the fish to an opening and then trapping them inside. It doesn't involve a person being there which may prove beneficial. Basically you just have to set up the trap.

You have to be very prayerful when setting up a spiritual trap. This happened to me before. A man called me and shared that he was having trouble with his sons. Since I was younger than the father, I had a rapport with young men. The Lord used me as a trapping mechanism. Think of trapping as interventions when people desperately need help. You are able to go talk to them and tell them about Jesus Christ. You try to get them to a place where they will listen to you. The set up has been put in place and preparation has been made ahead of time to get the person from point A to point B. We know the route, we just need to get the person there. When you are trapping, there is not a certain age group, but it is usually people that you have some influence over. Sharing your testimony when you have been in similar situations can cause a turn around in those you are witnessing to. You can say things such as, "I see the direction you are headed in. Believe me you don't want to go there. I've been there."

Trapping is not meant to be a lot of work with a lot of bait, but basically just set it up and give your testimony of what God has done for you and what He has brought you through.

In the Bible Jonah, who was already a servant of God, had to be trapped by God Himself. God told Jonah to go to Nineveh, but he decided to go to Tarshish instead. Jonah went to sleep and woke up to find that the boat is in a terrible storm because of him. The others on the boat threw him overboard, and he was swallowed by a big fish that God had prepared just for him. He was trapped in the fish for three days with no way out until his intervention was over. God wanted to use Jonah to preach repentance, but he didn't want to do this. God had to use the trapping technique so that Jonah could go forth and use the netting technique on the people of Nineveh. (Jonah 1)

Chapter 4: Preparing Equipment

Before you begin to fish, you need to make sure you have everything you need beforehand. Preparation is very key to catching fish. Let's look at a checklist of the things you need. Later we will go more in depth about this equipment.

1.   **A boat.** People close to shore are those who have some understanding of God and know what He is capable of, but have strayed away from the church because of being hurt by people or allowing sin to creep into their daily lives (backsliders). For whatever reason, they have allowed Satan to bamboozle them. They still hang close to the shore because it is familiar, but they have not allowed the Holy Spirit to come into their lives to keep them. Some people, however you will need to go beyond the shore to reach. They are not going to come close enough to the shore for you to catch. You will have to use your boat.

2.   **A net.** Jesus didn't fish with a fishing pole, and you will notice He told the disciples to cast their net. When you use a pole, you are only looking for a certain kind of fish. Don't get me wrong there will be times when you witness to only one person at a time and that is a good thing. But when you are trying to reach the multitudes, you need a net. A fishing rod has only one hook, so there is no way you are going to catch

more than one fish at a time. That is why Jesus told His disciples to use a net. Net brings to mind two words, network and Internet. The meaning of net is bringing something together…something enclosed, something covered, or something caught. Most people realize that when you **network,** you have a group of resources   that has been grouped together. You don't have to search far because it is right there. People surf the **Internet**. A lot of information is right there at your fingertips. It has been collected and grouped together in a net. So whether you speak about network, Internet, or net worth you speak about something that has been drawn together.

       3.   **Bait.** You absolutely need bait. Bait is very important because it lures fishes to the proper position to be caught. In the spiritual realm, the bait we use gets people in the position to accept Jesus as their personal Savior.

       4.   **The Catch holding.** Where are you going to keep the fishes before you make it back to the shore? How will you keep them from spoiling? These questions have to be answered before catching the fish.

       5.   **Patience.** This cannot be purchased at the grocery store, on Amazon,

or at a bait and tackle shop. This can only come from God.

Chapter 5: The Boat

Now let's do a breakdown of why we need these things. Why do we need a boat to fish? Let's examine Luke the fifth chapter. Jesus is being introduced to His first disciples (although He already **knew** them, they didn't know Him). People were anxious to hear the Word of God. Jesus saw two boats and decided that He needed to use one of those boats. He asked Simon who owned one of the boats if he would steer his boat a little way from land. He needed to get just a little bit away from the crowd to be better heard. He went about His Father's business as He used the boat for His pulpit and began to teach the people. Apparently, the people on the shore were souls that had already been caught by Jesus. He was teaching them and giving them information about God. Jesus was actually preaching to the church. As I said before, the ones on the shore are the ones who know "church". You don't have to launch out into the deep because they are right there at the edge. Many times you will find people that have distanced themselves from God. All they need is to be reassured that God loves them. It is easy for them to come back because God will show Himself as you begin to minister. Sometimes you have to be off the land just for a little way to grab those people just as Jesus did in this passage of scripture. They are right there at the shore of salvation, so close to the safety zone that they can reach out and touch it. These people are lost, but only need to be reminded that God loves them.

After Jesus finished teaching and preaching to the ones on shore, He asked Simon to go out into the deep water. In order to launch out into the deep you need to be in a boat because you can't swim and catch fish at the same time. What is your boat? Your boat can be your car or your feet. Your boat is simply the mode of transportation you use to get to the souls that God has assigned you. Your mode of transportation can be your forklift on your job or an airplane that you're on when you're going to preach on the other side of the world. It can be a train ride or a ride on a motorcycle with friends. God can even use wheelchairs and hospital beds as your boats. How can God use you if you are in a hospital bed? I'm glad you asked. A lady shared with me a revelation that the Holy Spirit gave her. When you go therefore to preach to the world, it is not always a physical going. Sometimes you go in the spirit realm. So your voice can also become a boat. Your boat can be anything that will get you from one point to another point because most times you can't fish where you're comfortable. You can't stay inside your home to fish. You've got to leave your comfort zone, that place of familiarity. So whether you're on two wheels, four wheels, six wheels, eighteen wheels, or no wheels, if you use it to go where God leads you to fish, that is your boat.

When Jesus asked Simon to go into the deep, we can almost hear Simon asking, "Why, Lord? Come on, now. Why do we need to go out into the deep?" And Jesus replying, "Because I want to show you something." Sometimes God wants to show you **Who He Is.** But sometimes in order for God to show you who He is, He has to take you into unfamiliar territory. Your boat is going to take you away from your comfort zone. It is going to take you to the places and communities that need to know Jesus Christ. Your boat will take you to remote villages and to crack houses. Your boat will take you to those small children who need Jesus. We all need a boat to take us to the souls that God has assigned to us.

I'm going to share a secret about myself, so please don't tell anyone. I am not too fond of actual boats. I am not comfortable being on a boat in deep water. Since I am not a strong swimmer, I am not confident in myself. I don't trust my ability to get back to shore if something happens to that boat. So sometimes God has to get us out there in that which is unfamiliar to us, so that our confidence is not in ourselves, but in Him.

In the sixth chapter of Genesis we see how the boat has played an important part in ministry since the beginning of time:

5 The LORD saw how great the wickedness of the human race had become on the earth, and that every inclination of the thoughts of the human heart was only evil all the time.

6 The LORD regretted that he had made human beings on the earth, and his heart was deeply troubled. 7 So the LORD said, "I will wipe from the face of the earth the human race I have created—and with them the animals, the birds and the creatures that move along the ground—for I regret that I have made them."

8 But Noah found favor in the eyes of the LORD.

In the first book of the Bible, Genesis, chapter 7:1-2 (NIV) God speaks to Noah. "Go into the ark, you and your whole family, because I have found you righteous in this generation. Take with you seven pairs of every kind of clean animal, a male and its mate, and one pair of every kind of unclean animal, a male and its mate". God instructed Noah to build an ark so that he and his family would be safe from the flood that he was sending to destroy the earth. He instructed him to use gopher wood and to put rooms in the ark using pitch within and without. So God was very specific with what He wanted Noah to do.

Webster defines a boat as a vessel for traveling on water. If you will notice, God's instructions to Noah to build the ark came early in the Bible. That makes us realize that if the boat was so important then, it is still important now in the year 2019. You need a way to get from Point A to Point B. What does a boat have to do with evangelizing? I'm glad you asked. As I mentioned, your boat gets you from Point A to Point B. What causes your boat to move? Your body! In the natural our bodies can move without a boat, but a boat cannot move unless a body causes it to move. In the spiritual realm your body is the power that propels the boat.

Therefore, I urge you brothers and sisters, in view of God's mercy to offer your bodies as a living sacrifice, holy and pleasing to God. This is your proper worship. (Romans 12:1 NIV) Paul is letting us know that our bodies are boats (vessels) that travel through the earth trying to warn people just as Noah tried to warn of the flood that was coming to destroy the earth. God sent a rainbow as His promise that He would not destroy the earth by water again, but He will destroy it by fire. Your body is the vessel that the Holy Spirit resides in. When you get in a boat and go out into the deep, you are trusting that the boat will not fail you. So we trust our bodies to take us from Point A to Point B. God is not going to use a vessel that is not willing to be used. You have to be willing and you have to allow yourself to be used by God. A lot of people don't understand that in order to evangelize, you must first yield yourself. You have never seen

God's hand reach down from Heaven to do His work. He does it through vessels—through His people. When we yield ourselves as willing vessels, God is edified. He is exalted through our boats, our bodies. One thing that we can say about a boat that it is not going anywhere unless you take it there. Every boat has to have a captain. That captain maneuvers the boat from east to west, from north to south. That captain puts in longitude and latitude coordinates to get to where he wants to take the boat. He makes sure that the boat stays on course and reaches its destination at the proper time. When you present your body as a living sacrifice, God becomes the Captain of your boat. When we didn't know Christ we were just floating in the ocean without any direction. We were living our lives however we wanted to live them, and we allowed life to take us in any direction by the wind and the waves. But when we presented our bodies holy and pleasing unto God, we moved our agendas out of the way and allowed God to take residence in our bodies and navigate them to do His work on this earth. You have permission to not let Him take control. You have permission to say, "I don't want Him to reside in me." When you accept Christ you turn your agenda over to Him, and you allow Him to do whatever He wants with the vessel that He designed anyway. The Bible says that you were made from the dust of the earth. God made you just as He made Adam. He made your ark. He gave Noah instructions on how to build his ark in Genesis 6:16. He told him to make it 300 cubits long, 15 cubits wide, and 30 cubits high. So being that God was very specific with Noah there had to be a plan and a purpose. He knew exactly what He needed on the boat to get His agenda fulfilled. I said that to say this: God had a plan when He designed you! He knew what things you would encounter. He knew that sometimes the waves would try to overtake you. He knew all of that, so He built and designed you a certain way. He already knew the course that He was going to have to take you through in order for Him to be glorified and to get the glory out of your life. Your body is your boat. That's how you are traveling on this earth.

Once your body has been presented as a living sacrifice, it no longer belongs to you. Anything that you sacrifice no longer belongs to you. Let me say that again. Anytime you present something as a sacrifice, it is the same as presenting a gift. Once that gift leaves your hands you have no authority over it any longer. I like what Paul asked the Corinthian Church. Do you not know that your bodies are temples (vessels) of the Holy Spirit, who is in you, whom you have received from God? You are not your own. (I Corinthians 6:19 NIV) You were bought with a price; therefore, honor God with your bodies. Get this: this is why you are a boat. When you give Him your life, your heart He becomes the captain of your vessel, your boat. And because He is the Captain He lives in you. Christ paid the price for your body. He paid the price for your life over 2,000 years ago. So being that you have accepted Him as your personal Savior, He has taken residence inside of you. Since He is the captain of your boat, He now tells you where to go. He may speak to me and say, "Daniel, I want you to go to the grocery store. And while you are there doing what you need to do, I want you to use every opportunity to help someone." God doesn't want to consume our lives. "The thief comes only to steal and kill and destroy; I have come that they may have life, and have it to the full." (John 10:10 NIV) God wants you to enjoy your life, but as you are enjoying your life, the thief is going to come in and try to swindle and bamboozle you. But if you allow me to take up residence in you and guide you, it won't matter what the enemy tries to do. With me, not only will you have life, but you will have life more abundantly. All God needs from you is to let Him have opportunity. He wants to use your day to day living as an example to others because you are the boat doing evangelism. Just as God knew what storms would come with Noah, He knows what storms will come with you. And since He promised to keep Noah safe, He built the ark with that promise in mind. In order to keep you from hurt, harm and danger He also has to know what your vessel can withstand. That is why the heart attack didn't kill you. That's why when I was diagnosed with transverse myelitis and would be paralyzed from the waist down never to walk again, God said "No! Because I live inside of you and need to use you, I can't allow what the doctors say to affect you. I have other plans for your life."

The boat is a very important tool in evangelism and everyone has to have a vessel in order to fish. You are the vessel that has to go down to those neighborhoods in your community. You are the boat that goes in the stores. You are the boat that goes on vacation. In your everyday living you are the vessel being used as you go through life's journey. Bishop Ronald E. Brown said, "There's a storm out on the ocean and it's moving this a way. If your soul's not anchored in Jesus it will surely drift away." I understand what Bishop Brown is saying because if your soul is not anchored in Jesus you can easily drift out into the ocean. A ship without a sail just drifts aimlessly. In conclusion, your body is your boat getting you from Point A to Point B—crossing the bridge, crossing the ocean, crossing the street, crossing the highway, crossing the highway. In other words wherever you are. You are the vessel that the Holy Spirit resides in and uses to be God's hands and feet. Are you willing to let God be the captain of your boat?

Chapter 6: The Net

Once again, the Kingdom of Heaven is like a net that was let down into the lake and caught all kinds of fish. When it was full, the fishermen pulled it up on the shore. Then they sat down and collected the good fish in baskets, but threw the bad away. This is how it will be at the end of age. The angels will come and separate the wicked from the righteous and throw them into the blazing furnace, where there will be weeping and gnashing of teeth. (Matthew 13: 47-50 NIV)

In this passage of scripture Jesus is talking, actually He is preaching. Everyone knows that Jesus often used parables. The fact that Jesus referred to the net so many times in the New Testament lets us know how important He considered it. In that era of time, fishing was an important way of life. It was a way to make a living; in fact, three of the twelve disciples were fishermen. Jesus used what was familiar to the disciples and those around them to teach them. Today the church will often use a fishing pole because it is trying to attract only certain type of people. The net is like the kingdom of Heaven. It is not like a denomination nor a particular age group. Jesus is referring to everybody. That is why you have to use a net because you are not fishing for a particular people. You are fishing for all kinds of souls. The scripture tells us that all kinds of fish were caught, big fish, little, fish, bass, flounder, mullets, crabs. Anything under the ocean was subject to being caught. That is how the Kingdom of God is. It is a net. Jesus is explaining to the people here like, "Listen, I am searching for everyone here who has a soul. I'm looking for anyone who was born of a woman. I am searching for anyone who will let me come in. Behold, I stand at the door and knock. If anyone hears my voice and opens the door, I will come in to him and eat with him, and he with me." Jesus is talking to everybody. It likes throwing a net on the side of the boat. When you throw your net out, make sure it is laying flat on the water so it is more effective. You want to make sure it catches fish while it is going to the bottom of the ocean. The net is important because it catches a multitude of fishes at one time. We need this in evangelism. Luke 5:4 reads, When He had finished speaking He said to Simon, "Launch out into the deep, and let your nets down for a draught." He understands that they don't want to catch fish in the shallow water. As I mentioned in a previous chapter, the ones in the shallow water are the ones that have been around church and know church but have backslidden. But the ones in the deep are the ones that have never been in the shallow water before. They are the ones that are in the deep waters where no one can find them. No one can see them. They don't hear the good news of Jesus Christ every day. Maybe they don't have social media. They don't have Trinity Broadcasting Network, the largest

Christian broadcasting network in the world. They are out there in jungles and villages and Jesus is just wanting us to get beyond ourselves, get out of our comfort zones, and launch out into the deep and cast our nets.

If you will notice, fish travel in a group. That group travels in schools. A lot will travel together at a particular time. There will be times when you will have the opportunity to evangelize to a whole group of people at one time just as Billy Graham and Reinhard Bonnke did when they were evangelizing. They had opportunities to reach so many souls at one time because the people were so hungry. They didn't know about Jesus Christ, but they knew something was lacking in their lives. They wanted a new way of living. They knew there had to be a better way. The evangelists presented Jesus to a mass of people and when they presented Him, not just one came but many came.

After Jesus' death and resurrection, Peter preached to the masses and 3000 souls were saved and added to the church. (Acts 2:41) He used a net to pull that school of fish together. Why is a net so important? The net does three things and I want you to get this. Number one it **covers.** It covers a portion of the ocean and then it goes down and it **catches** those things that are in the way of the net. Then it **encloses.** The net brings everything together so that it can be pulled to shore. The Bible tells us in the parable about the net that it caught all kinds of fishes and when it was full the fishermen pulled it to shore. When you throw the net it will come back full. The fishermen had to pull the net to shore. The shore can be on your boat or the shoreline of the ocean. The shore can be at your desk or in your car, the pool or the grocery line. The shore can be anywhere. The shore is when you get something close to you and you are able to maneuver it because it is out of its habitat. It will not be able to function because it is out of its league. You've heard the saying "like a fish out of water". So now you have brought the fish in your area. In the parable the fishermen sat down and put the good fish in the basket. There will be times when you preach to the masses, that everyone will not come. When you make a big catch, some will come just to bring trouble and they will be put out. But the net is meant to catch a lot of fish.

So if you are going to fish, you have to have a net. There will be times that you will encounter a group of people who are searching for a new way of life. The Bible says, "Let everything that has breath praise the Lord". (Psalm 150) That means if they have breath in their bodies, if they have a heartbeat, Jesus wants to have a relationship with them. So that means we are not looking for a particular economic status or a particular educational status or a particular skin color. We're looking for everyone who has a heartbeat and has blood running warm in their veins. Whether they are young or old, whatever they may be involved in, God loves them. He sent His only begotten Son, Jesus Christ, to die for their sins so that they should not perish but have everlasting life. They need to know this. That's why we go out into the deep and launch there. If we go into the deep, we will find ourselves in treacherous water sometimes. We might find ourselves in uncomfortable situations sometimes, but that does not mean we stop working or casting our nets. It is so important that we get every fish under the net. In the spiritual realm this means we lead every soul we can to Christ.

When I was in India they told me about the village that did not have the life- giving church. Later on in the book, I'll get into this a little deeper. We began to set up. I made the altar call and told the people that Jesus loves them. Before I told them about Jesus, all they knew was Hinduism. But they were ready for change. They knew they were getting the same results in life even though they tried new things. They wanted to hear more about this living God…this God that could hear them and comfort them. As we gave the invitation to them to accept Jesus as their personal Savior many flocked to the altar. The net was thrown out there. Jesus said the kingdom of Heaven is like a net. When it is let down on the lake it catches all kinds of fishes. Our spiritual net catches men, women, little boys, and little girls who have the desire to give their hearts to Jesus Christ.

Now grabbing a lot of fish at one time takes a lot more work than if you are just pole fishing for one particular fish. When you cast your net, you can't pull all of those fish on your boat by yourself. You are going to need help. This work is not meant to be done alone. But when you cast your nets, your nets have little weights on the bottom that widen and allow the net to lay flat on the water and go down to the bottom quickly. The net is able to pull back what is caught in the net. Now, many of us have been fishing with nets but we've been catching the wrong things. What do I mean by that? You've been catching seaweed. You've been catching things that are not living and that have no value above the ocean. It is more of a treasure hunt than fishing for souls. But we need to understand there are valuable souls, valuable people out there who need to know that God loves them.

Your net is simply your mouth. The Bible tells us that life and death is in the power of the tongue. Your mouth is that net that you speak what God wants you to speak. Words are spirits. Once they are put in the atmosphere they have the power to change lives forever. Whether it is one life or 10,000 or 20,000 lives, let your net work. That's is why we need to understand that there is power in your mouth. So stop speaking negatively. Stop speaking death, speak life. This is what Jesus was referring to in His parable. People are drawn to your words when you speak life. Your net is right there on you. I want to encourage you to use it. Where do you use your net? You can use your net at work, walking down the street, walking on the trail. You can use your net while standing in line to buy ice cream. Whenever or wherever the opportunity arises, your net is ready to be used. All you have to do is open your mouth! When your mouth speaks love, people are drawn to Christ. He tells you exactly where to cast your net. There are souls waiting on you.

Chapter 7: The Bait

Bait is also important when fishing. In fact, I would say that it is one of the most essential things you need to fish. Bait is used to lure the fish to a position where they will be caught. In the spiritual realm bait is used to get people in the position to accept Jesus Christ as their personal Savior.

In the natural there are so many types of bait and you use the bait that attracts the fish that you want to catch. We know that bait is important in the spiritual realm because Jesus used it as He walked the earth. As you know, Jesus performed miracles. The miracles served as bait to catch people's attention. That is the purpose of bait—to draw people's attention. It entices people to draw a little closer. As a matter of fact we use bait all of the time. If you look in the newspaper every day and especially on Sunday, you will see coupons. Those coupons are bait to make people want to come to certain stores to shop. Commercials, YouTube, and informercials are all written to capture your attention. Billboards, signs, and personalized license tags draw your attention while you are traveling. All of those things are bait meant to lure you in. Our mailboxes are filled with fliers and offers of easy credit. Bait tempts us to try something new or to try something again.

Just as bait draws the fish to a place where it can be caught, Jesus also drew people to Him all through His ministry as He performed miracles. People witnessed the miracles and said, "Wow! How did He do that? Is He a prophet? He is healing the sick and raising the dead! Who is this man that can feed 5000 people?" And that is how the bait was used—to make their minds wonder what manner of man is this among us? He did things to shock them. Sometimes in order to get people's attention, you have to do things that are out of the ordinary.

When Jesus was on the earth He was such a smooth operator. In Matthew 5:29-30 Jesus says shocking things -- telling His listeners to pluck out their eyes or cut off their hands to keep their bodies from sinning. Jesus didn't really mean for anyone to do this, but He wanted to keep them intrigued. He wanted them to wonder about what He said and to investigate it further. He was throwing out bait.

Let me tell you one thing about Jesus. Before He met the spiritual needs of His followers and listeners, He first met their physical needs. How can you receive anything spiritually from someone if you have a natural need? That is why He tells us that love draws people. Most of the time people come to receive Jesus Christ in their lives in either of two times in their lives. They come through tragedy or through transition. Maybe there has been a death in the family, a divorce or breakup or maybe there has been a big move or change. Those two T's—tragedy or transition draws people in because they are more vulnerable during these times. And that's why we have to show the love of Christ to them during these times. If you look back and think about your own salvation, chances are you were either going through a tragedy or a transition.

I was saved as a young man, but as I got older I became disconnected from church. I was a teenager out in the world enjoying life, enjoying the "sinning" life. Then my brother was killed, and that tragedy brought me back to a place with God. I realized that there was a void inside of me that I could not fill; only Christ could fill it. So I came back to Christ because of a tragedy. If you will look back at your whole life, really look back, you will remember coming to Christ when you were going through a transition. You were trying to find yourself, trying to find love, moving somewhere that you didn't have loved ones living, or you experienced a tragedy as I did. God allows those opportunities and then He allows bait to come draw you in.

Let me tell you something. Jesus was one of the "baddest" preachers on earth. He knew how to reach people and draw them in. He was a wonderful storyteller and told countless parables. He pulled spiritual truths from everyday life. Not only did those stories make Jesus's preaching more memorable, they also connected in much more profound ways. Look at the parable of the prodigal son. Jesus proclaimed that God loves you so much that He will welcome you back to Him no matter how far you have wandered away. This is true. God does love His people that much. Jesus used stories like that because He wanted the people to see how much God loved them, and He loves us that same way today. Jesus told the story of how a young man partied away his inheritance and came home begging for mercy. Surprisingly he was welcomed back with open arms because his daddy had been waiting for his return every day that he was away. What is even more powerful is when you want to preach like Jesus you have to tell the stories. Use examples of everyday life as spiritual teachings.

When you use bait and begin to talk to people, tell stories about yourself. Tell stories about your life. Tell about your downfalls and how you overcame them. We, as Christians, can be more relatable if we learn to be "real" with people about some of the struggles we went through and came through. Those seeking Christ will look at you and realize that you know exactly what they are going through. I love telling stories, even when I am preaching. I incorporate life stories because let me tell you something, people can relate to them. They can find who they are in the story.

As I said, Jesus was a wonderful storyteller who often shocked people by the things He said. Jesus also asked questions. A lot of times when we talk to people we want to do all of the talking. Sometimes it is best to just listen. That's how you make conversation by asking questions. I had an opportunity to have a conversation with a Jehovah's Witness. I sat and listened as he tried to convert me, but I stayed true to what I believe without arguing. The Word is true all by itself and you don't have to argue about your belief. Let people tell you what they believe because you know who God is. When you listen to them and show concern for them, you catch their attention. After he finished talking, I had the opportunity to talk and to witness to him. When I was finished, he accepted Christ. Had I not listened to him, chances are he would not have listened to me. That is bait. Most of the time people just need an ear to listen and an opportunity to express themselves and to tell someone what is going on in their lives.

When you go fishing you have to know what bait to use. Sometimes your bait is listening. Sometimes it is telling a story. Sometimes your bait is filling a natural need such as hunger. When I was in India, we had done our homework concerning the village where I was going to preach the gospel. We took cookies and drinks because they were not financially stable enough to buy those kinds of treats for themselves. So during the crusade we handed out cookies and juice boxes and they sat there and ate and drank as they listened to the Word of God. It humbled them to know that someone loved them enough to give them something without expecting anything in return. We don't have to charge for everything. Jesus never charged. Sometimes we just have to do things from out of the goodness of our hearts. At Life Springs Church we have something called "something extra cards". They are cards inviting people to church. When you go through a drive through you give the cashier the card to give to the next person in line. Whoever receives the card is also informed that the meal has been paid for. The card does two things. It supplies a natural need and also a spiritual need because it is our way of letting people know, if they don't already know, that God loves them. Look at how simple that is. I have never seen the hand of God physically. He uses people like you and me to help people. It can be offering someone a ride or taking a meal to someone who is homeless or anything you do without expecting something in return.

The purpose of bait is to lure people to a certain place. We want to aspire them. Once you aspire a person then you can inspire them. God uses your life as bait for someone who is going through transition or tragedy. Once you know what your purpose and plan is, you can aspire people. Once they are inspired they can then inspire others.

It is a continuous cycle. Jesus took 12 disciples and taught them and now look at the world today. Many people all over the world celebrating Christ because of Who He Is! And it started with Him using bait.

Let me explain something about bait. I want to bring something to your attention. Some people you try to reach will not want to be reached beyond what you can do for them in the natural. Look at John 6 starting at the 22nd verse.

22 The next day the crowd that had stayed on the opposite shore of the lake realized that only one boat had been there, and that Jesus had not entered it with his disciples, but that they had gone away alone.

23 Then some boats from Tiberias landed near the place where the people had eaten the bread after the Lord had given thanks.

24 Once the crowd realized that neither Jesus nor his disciples were there, they got into the boats and went to Capernaum in search of Jesus.

25 When they found him on the other side of the lake, they asked him, "Rabbi, when did you get here?"

26 Jesus answered, "Very truly I tell you, you are looking for me, not because you saw the signs I performed but because you ate the loaves and had your fill.

27 Do not work for food that spoils, but for food that endures to eternal life, which the Son of

Man will give you. For on him God the Father has placed his seal of approval."

These people are looking for Jesus because He had fed them physically and they wanted something else to eat. You will find people that will only want what you can give them. Even Jesus realized that some people will only want the physical food and not care to be fed spiritually. But He let them know that He could not continue to take care of their physical needs only. Please take note of that and use your bait wisely. Do your homework. If you go into a place that has a lot of children, try to reach the children. When you reach people's children, you will reach them. Find out if a family has a specific need and try to meet that need. And always take the opportunity to share the good news of Jesus Christ. Your bait is important. Again, use it wisely.

Chapter 8: The Catch Holding

We've come down to one of the final moments of fishing. I want to share with you one of the last things you are going to need; however, you are going to need this before you catch your first fish. What you must decide on and have in mind is what you are going to do with the fish after you catch it. You have to know how you are going to handle it. The fish has to be kept somewhere before it is cleaned. As you fish for souls you have to be prepared at all times as well. Let me note this before going any further: a fish can be cleaned and prepared in the natural, but when you fish for souls there is only One who can clean that soul. And that is Jesus Christ. It is not our job as believers and followers of Jesus Christ to try to fix anyone. I think we as believers have found ourselves in this dilemma or in the place that we feel it is our duty to do the cleaning. But Jesus is the only One! So now that we have established that, we can move on and find out how to be prepared for the catch. Go fishing expecting to reap a harvest.

Serious bowlers never go to the bowling alley without their bowling balls. Basketball players find out beforehand if the gym supplies balls. If not, they take their own basketball. So it is with fishing for souls. You have to take your equipment with you. What do you do when you have either launched out into the deep and used your nets or used your fishing poles or used your hands—whatever method you have used to catch fish—what do you do after the catch? Let me tell you this. What you do **not** want to do is try to clean your fish on the boat. If you've ever tried to clean a fish on the boat or on the pier you soon found out the fish was still slippery. It still had enough power left to try to get back into the water. Cleaning a fish near its habitat is not a good idea because it can easily make its way back into the water and swim far away from you. In the future the fish will be more cautious and wiser about getting caught. The fish is now damaged and wounded returning to the water without any first aid. Underneath the water there is no hospital or doctor to treat those wounds. The fish will carry that scar for a lifetime just because it was not handled correctly.

There is something called a mesh wire which is simply a basket designed to keep your catch alive. If you want fresh fish, you want to keep the fish alive after you get it on the boat. This basket has self-closing mechanisms. Attached to the wire mesh is a rope that hangs into the water with enough room for the fish to swim freely. The fish is still in its habitat but is living in an enclosed bubble and being guided in this wire mesh. So the fish is probably thinking that while he is still in his habitat, he is now only going in a certain direction.

Now let's look at that from a spiritual standpoint. When fishing for souls we find out that

God has used us to draw a person and that person is getting closer to acceptance. When we get a catch as fishers of men don't take the catch away from the habitat before it is time, causing damage. Think about the people you have caught as being in a wire mesh basket being led and guided, hearing the voice of the fisher because they are now closer to the boat. In their minds they are thinking, "I'm still in my habitat; I am okay." What you do now is build relationships. This is meeting someone right where they are. When you are building relationships, the first conversation does not have to be about Jesus Christ. Talk about the football game, talk about the basketball game, talk about common interests before offering Christ. Most people understand that a relationship is built up before introducing Jesus Christ. So you've made the catch, now you want to build up the relationship. As you put effort into the relationship, that person will begin to trust you and see something different inside of you. They will start to want whatever it is that you have on the inside that makes you different. Now you have encouraged them, you have ignited something in them to make them want something bigger and better than they have. What is bigger and better than what they already have? We all know. It is Jesus Christ! So this gives us the opportunity to have relationships with them. Sometimes you are on the same team with them, the same fraternity, a civic group or organization. Maybe your children play on the same little league team. The bottom line is to build relationships wherever you go. Let me tell you something, if you are going to be a fisher of men, you have to be a lover of people. Fishers build relationships and with these relationships they know the importance of understanding where people are.

We've talked about keeping natural fish alive on the boat in order to keep them fresh. How does this translate to being fishers of men? We don't want to kill the spirit of people with thoughtless actions and words. This goes along with meeting people where they are. If you run into drug addicts, meet them where they are. You can check on them and tell them you want to make sure they are okay. You can take them out for a meal. If you show the love of Christ and learn how to build relationships, you will be amazed at how easy it is to lead someone to Christ. Learn to let people be people and meet them where they are.

We as people want to change others to be more like ourselves. But we are not to be judges. There is only One Righteous Judge. Being that He is the only One, it is not our duty nor our right to try to clean somebody or to try to judge somebody. Learn to say, "You know what? Even though they are drug addicts who may be high or may be drunk, I am going to love them anyway. I am going to meet them where they are." You can easily build relationships with them because they know you love them unconditionally and are not just trying to win their souls. You should try to build a relationship with every soul that you are trying to win, especially when it is one on one. Maybe you have children that go to karate together and you sit together as you wait for the lesson to be over. Maybe you know a mom who is a single mom and she is going through some things. Simply giving her a thinking of you card will uplift her day. Or maybe you want to give her a gift card to Chick-Fil-A or Subway to give her a night off from cooking. When you love people where they are, they will begin to talk to you. They will begin to share their lives with you. When they begin to share their lives, they are giving you information that will help you build the case for Jesus Christ that you may be able to persuade them. When I witness to others, I think of myself as a lawyer inside of the courtroom trying to convince the jury that Jesus is Lord. That's my job.

As you are fishing, you have to realize you need to keep your fish alive. The way to keep them alive is to put them in the wire mesh locked in and submerge them under the water. They are still in their natural habitat, but they are being led and guided to where they need to go. So just don't run up and take someone out of their environment. If you ease them out of that place of darkness, out of that place of bitterness, out of that place of depression, you can easily lead them to a better place. When I talk about moving them from places, most of the time it is not moving them from a physical place; it is moving them from places of despair within themselves. But you first have to meet them where they are.

When you go fishing you have to decide where you are going to put your catch. Most people keep fish on a stringer in the water while they continue to fish. Sometimes I go to my daughter's school and they have to hold onto a rope to keep them in line and to keep them together. That's what a stringer does, it keeps the fish together. It does not allow them to get separated and ease back into the water.

If I were to flip this over to the spiritual side, I would stress building relationships so that you can lead your catch out of the place they are in. I want to share a scripture text because Jesus gave us a good example of this in John the fourth chapter beginning at the seventh verse. Jesus met a Samaritan woman at a well. Jesus was Jewish, and the Jewish people and the Samaritans did not have dealings with one another in that region during that time. Samaritans were considered to be in a lower class. This woman also had a history, a background. Whether you know it or not, we all have a history of something we are not proud of, something we are ashamed of. This woman, like everyone else, had a history. Jesus first asked her if she would draw him a drink of water from the well. Jesus is not asking her for water because He considers her beneath Him, He is opening the door for a relationship. He wants to talk with her and meet her right where she is. She feels worthless, unworthy, not measuring up to the status of a Jew. You can imagine her outward look and appearance reflect how down on herself she is. Now here comes Jesus, a Jew, who society had decided was of a higher class of people, asking for a drink of water. Now let's use our imaginations for a moment. If you and someone else are the only two people at the well, you're not going to be mean and say, "No, I am not going to give you any water." You are not going to pretend not to hear the request. After all, it is just the two of you there. It's so easy to have a conversation and to put differences aside. So when Jesus asks for the water she responds "Why do you want this water from me? The Jews don't have dealings with Samaritans." The woman notices that Jesus doesn't even have anything to put the water in. Nevertheless, she gives Jesus the water. Jesus then starts talking to her about living water telling her that with the natural water she will thirst again, but He can give her water and she will never thirst again. She wonders what kind of water causes you never to thirst again. Was it there at Jacob's well? This water was drunk by Jacob's family and his cattle. What is better than this? Aquafina? Deer Park? If it's better than that, I want some of it. Jesus begins to minister to her. He begins to tell her about her life. He asks her if she is married to which she answers in the negative. Jesus then surprises her by telling her she spoke the truth. Although she had been married five times, the man she is presently with is not her husband. The conversation seems to be going pretty well between two people that ordinarily would not have dealings with one another. Jesus understands that He has to keep her in her habitat, but He wants to change the way she thinks about herself. He wants her to go in another direction. He doesn't try to clean her up, He challenges her. He lets her know who He is. He lets her know that He is the Messiah, the King of Kings and the Lord of Lords. Now she understands that she has had an encounter with Jesus Christ. She understands about the living water. She is so excited that she had this encounter that when the disciples come back to where Jesus is, she leaves her water bucket at the well and goes to the city. She is ecstatic and wants everyone to come meet Jesus. "Come see a man." Jesus's one on one fishing has now led to the woman letting down the net. She has now become a fisher of souls.

Just as the Samaritan woman invited others, you too, will know when it is time to invite people to church. You might say, "Daniel, I can't. I don't feel comfortable leading people". But there is one thing I have found out, and that is if you can get people to the church, which is the holding place, the Word of God and the Holy Spirit will convict and persuade. Jesus is telling them to follow Him because He wants them to have a better life. He wants to clean them up. Your job is to lead by example rather than trying to point your finger at people telling them what they should or should not do. You don't reach people by telling them they are going to Hell. Let me stop you right there. Most people wouldn't wish their worst enemy in Hell, so if you don't wish it on your worst enemy, why would you wish anybody in Hell? You shouldn't do that. So you want to make sure you reach those people who are seeking to know God or those who are seeking a new way and don't know yet that it is Christ they are seeking. But you have to meet them right where they are.

Chapter 9: Patience

As we go through this manual you will find out that patience is written several times in many different forms. In fishing at the top of the list of things you need is not your bait nor what you are fishing with. It is your attitude. This is true when fishing in the natural and when fishing spiritually. You have to have a patient attitude. Webster defines patience as bearing pains or trials commonly without complaint; manifesting forbearance under provisional strain; not hasty; steadfast despite opposition, difficulties or adversities; able or willing to bear.

When fishing you have to know that patience is the key whether you're trying to catch a big fish, a small fish, a crab, an oyster or any living thing under the ocean. In order to lure them to a place to be caught, you have to have patience.

The Bible tells us the fruit of the Spirit is love, joy, peace, **patience**, gentleness, goodness, faith, meekness, and temperance. This is the fruit you need to be effective in your everyday life and very needful when fishing for souls. Today we live in a microwave society and a lot of people do not have the patience to wait on things. We live in a world where we want instant results. We think about something today, but then realize we wanted it yesterday or the day before that-- before the thought was even formed or the words were spoken from our lips. We have a "right now" mentality. I think that society has put us in a position that if it's possible to get something without waiting for it, we go ahead and get it.

Habakkuk 2:3 reads, "For the vision is yet for an appointed time, but at the end it shall speak, and not lie: though it tarry, wait for it; because it will surely come, it will not tarry." There is power in waiting and while waiting you need patience. The Bible tells us in Philippians 4:6-7, "Do not be anxious about anything, but in every situation, by prayer and petition, with thanksgiving, present your requests to God. And the peace of God, which transcends all understanding, will guard your hearts and your minds in Christ Jesus."

A lot of times when we get things too quickly we don't value them as much because we think we did something on our own. When I was growing up my parents did not give my siblings and me money out of their pockets. We did chores for our spending money. We valued that money more because we worked for it. It takes patience to find and land the large fish. Most of the time you will not be one of the ones fishing from the pier. If you are easily bored or have ADHD, as I do, you tend to want things instantly but again, you have to have patience. I would advise carrying a small tacklebox that you can set up because at any given moment the fish can be ready to bite. If you give up and walk away because the fish are not biting, you might lose the opportunity. The moment you walk away could very well be the time that they are ready to bite.

I remember a time that I went fishing with my grandfather and my dad. We sat around this pond for hours without a single bite. I was so bored. I was young and anxious to see some fish, but they just weren't cooperating. We just kept sitting and waiting and sitting and waiting some more. We would throw our lines out and the fish would nibble at the bait just enough to not get caught. It was as if they were toying with us. I will never forget that experience of sitting there all day in anticipation of catching a fish. But we didn't catch a thing. Storm clouds started gathering and my grandfather and my dad decided that we needed to leave. We packed our things up and left. After the storm passed, Daddy said "Let's go back and see if we can catch something now." My response, "Naw, I don't want to go back. We stayed down there all day and didn't catch anything." I stayed home because I knew going back was pointless. The two of them went back. Daddy later told me that as soon as they could get a fish off of one of the rods, there was a fish on the other line. That taught me a lesson on patience and in not giving up.

After storms fish come to the top of the water. As we talked about earlier, people often come to Christ after a tragedy or a transition. You have to be watchful because at any given moment the opportunity may present itself for you to catch that soul. Patience is key to fishing. You have to be able to sit there and wait. Sometimes you look around and everyone else seems to be catching fish. You feel like giving up, but you have to stay focused. Don't lose confidence in what you have thrown out into the water. The fish might just be ready to grab that bait just as you decide to give up.

Paul is a perfect example of patience in the Bible. In Ephesians 4 he wrote to the church at Ephesus. In this passage of scripture he is talking about unity and maturity in the body of believers. "As a prisoner for the Lord, then, I urge you to live a life worthy of the calling you have received. Be completely humble and gentle, be patient, bearing with one another in love" (verses 1 and 2 NIV). Paul's words are still true today. The calling we have received is to win souls for the Body of Christ. You have to be completely humble, gentle and patient if you are to win souls for Christ. In order to win souls you cannot have a haughty attitude. Treat people with love regardless of their circumstances. We talked about being relatable. If you approach people with the attitude that you are perfect and that you have always had it together, you will more than likely scare them away. You have to approach in a quiet, still manner. If you make the wrong move and lose that window of opportunity you will have to wait for another opportunity to come along. Meet people where they are in life and do not handle them in a rough manner. We don't know the hardships that people have been through. If a person is already wounded in spirit, being rough can cause irreversible damage. That is why we have to treat people gently and humbly as we witness to them

Jesus was gentle as He walked the earth. Even in His gentleness He was able to draw people in with love. He did not pressure, He did not push, He did not drag. We have to follow His example and lure people with our gentleness. Even as we are gentle, we must also practice patience. Patience is being steadfast despite opposition, despite difficulties or adversities. You will run into situations where you will come up against some opposition, where you will encounter difficulties and adversities. But you cannot allow that to deter you from your assignment. You cannot get caught up in your emotions or get caught up in self to the point that you forget about your ultimate goal and your ultimate assignment, which is to love one another and draw others in. So in Ephesians 4 Paul is talking to the church at Ephesus telling them to be gentle and patient and humble. And I want to encourage you to be the same as you go out to win souls. If you've been trying to win souls -- seeking and praying to God, you must also ask Him for patience.

You have to love people. Let me tell you something right now. There is no point to trying to win souls if you don't love people. Let's just take a quick check of our own salvation. As a matter of fact, you do realize that God *is* love? So if God is love and you serve Him, that means you represent love. So here is an important question: Do you have hatred in your heart? If so, I want you to take the time right now, right this second, don't wait another minute to repent. Pray "Lord, if there is any hatred in my heart that will prevent me from winning souls—that will keep me from being patient and from being humble—anything that will keep me from being loving, I ask you to remove it from my heart right now." If you read this sentence and repented, you have been forgiven of your sins as of this minute. So now you move forward past this. Win those souls that are lost.

One of my favorite scriptures is Galatians 6:9 where Paul is speaking to the church in Galatia. He is speaking about patience. "Let us not be weary in well doing. For in due season we shall reap if we faint not." Some of you have been patient and are doing all of the right things. You've been listening and showing love and asking God to lead and guide you. I can hear someone saying, "Daniel, I am doing all of those things. Why in the world is it not working for me? Why are people not coming to church? Why does it seem that no one is listening to my testimony? Why does it seem like my words are void, that I'm talking to myself? Just tell me why!" Paul's words warn us. He tells us not to be weary in doing good. Don't give up in doing good. Don't give in when you're doing good. You keep on doing the right things. Don't get weary in your well doing because there is a due season. For in the due season, you are going to reap. Yes, you are going to reach those souls that you have been planting seeds for. You are going to obtain those people. In due season, at the right time at the right moment when you feel like you are ready to throw up your hands and walk away, just press on and be persistent. In due season when God gets ready He will do the drawing. Yes, He uses you, but He does the drawing. In due season all the things you have planted will bloom. The people you thought were not listening will be ready to take the leap of faith. The people who only nibbled at the bait are ready to obtain greater things. In due season you shall reap only **if**—there is an if—you don't give up. If you don't give in. If you don't pull that hook in before time. If you don't let the net float away before the catch comes.

Sometimes it takes patience. Can I tell you something? It took a long time for you to get to where you are before God called you. It takes time. So don't give up on people because people didn't give up on you. So why should you give up on the lost souls out there? Every day you should be working on those who have been assigned to you. When you are fishing for souls, never have just one pole in the pond. My Daddy told me never to go fishing with just one pole. When you take just one, you lose out on fish that are ready to bite at the same time. So always have more than one hook inside the water. To recap: Don't be weary in well doing because in due season you will reap if you don't faint. Patience is the key. Without patience you will not reap the harvest. You won't reap what God has set up for you because you don't have the patience. One thing is for certain, you can not land a big catch without being patient. What you are doing is not in vain, but you have to stay persistent. Don't give up, don't walk away from it. You don't have to irritate people but always give them something to think about. Let them always know when they see you coming that you are going to speak life to them. You are always going to give them something good to take away from the conversation. Don't be the one who speaks negativity. When you are fishing for souls you don't want the people to know what the fisher is going through. You cannot fish for souls with a negative or *woe is me* attitude. You will not catch anyone.

You have to learn that patience is the key to a lot of things. Isaiah 40:31 tells us, "But they that wait upon the Lord shall renew their strength; they shall mount up with wings as eagles; They shall run, and not be weary; and they shall walk and not faint." But you have to be patient while you wait. You have to be able to be steadfast in difficulties and opposition. You have to be willing to bear. You have to endure hardships like a good soldier. You have to endure pain and endure rejection, and I think, make that I know, that people do not like being rejected. I'm going to be very real with you. Rejection was probably one of my biggest downfalls in finding myself. Any time you are rejected it is human nature to not want to risk being rejected again. The negative things people said about our dreams caused some of us not to fulfill that dream. When we were rejected in relationships, we thought less of ourselves. Most of us have had feelings of thinking we were flawed. Rejection plays with our minds so powerfully that it causes us not to have patience. We think that everyone has turned against us. But it is okay. When you are rejected just get back up and go again. The opposite of rejection is persistence. So if you get rejected, get persistent. Keep coming back with a different approach. What you want to do is keep feeding into that person you are trying to win over. Sometimes when you are fishing in the natural, fish are able to get the bait off of your hook and go back to the bottom of the ocean without getting caught. You are just feeding them for the next catch. We have to believe that the word of God does not go out void. Whatever He says He is going to do, that is what He is going to do. As fishers of men you have to have patience. Just remember someone had patience with you first.

Let me close this chapter with a story. When I was growing up I played football. My parents had eight children, so we could never play recreation sports because of the expense. My mother told us we could play on the school's football team. So when we got to middle school my brother and I started playing on the team. Now, mind you, I knew nothing about football. But when the coach saw that I was a big boy, he saw potential in me. He also knew that it would take patience to develop me into a good player. He kept working with me. I didn't know how to block, I didn't know anything about making a tackle. I was clueless about the rules of the game. But this coach had patience and didn't give up on me. He showed me all I needed to know about football and showed me how to use strategy on the field. His name is Coach Norton. That is a name I will never forget. He used patience to develop the potential he saw in me. He knew that we, as a team, would mess up sometimes. But he showed us the play again and had patience. When I got to high school I broke a record making nine touchdowns in one game. This was all because Coach Norton had patience and didn't give up. Because of his belief in me, I also had belief in myself. So I'm asking you not to give up on the people you are trying to win. They will mess up, they will fall, they will fail, but don't give up. Be persistent and keep moving. Remember patience is a key to winning souls.

Chapter 10

I hope you have gotten a lot of information about soul fishing in this manual. My prayer is that you will take this as a tool to help and motivate you to either become a better fisher or to begin fishing. The only way we can build the Kingdom of God is to come out of our comfort area and our comfort zone. We need to go beyond our households, go beyond our churches, and beyond our workplaces to find those who are dying and need to be revived back to life. You are the electrical currents that God uses to shock the hearts of dying people to bring them back to life. God cannot build His Kingdom without you. It is going to take everybody stepping out of the box and using every moment as an evangelistic moment to help bring people to Christ.

I believe and pray right now that God begins to open up your imagination and that He gives you all the tools, resources and networks that you need to take every moment of your life as a commercial for Jesus Christ. You are the hands and feet of God, and He needs you to fulfill His work here on earth.

I want to leave with you this small story. It is a parable that the Late John M. Drescher, wrote in April of 1979 when he was Minister of Scottdale Mennonite Church in Scottdale,

Pennsylvania. I believe this is a good note to close on 40 years after he wrote it. His words are still strong today, and I believe this is where we are headed in some of our churches. But we have to power to yield ourselves to Jesus Christ to have Him change us before we find ourselves in this predicament that I am about to share.

"A Fish Story" by John M. Drescher

Now it came to pass that a group existed who called themselves fishermen. And lo, there were many fish in the waters all around. In fact the whole area was surrounded by streams and lakes filled with fish. And the fish were hungry.

Week after week, month after month, and year after year these, who called themselves fishermen, met in meetings and talked about their call to fish, the abundance of fish, and how they might go about fishing. Year after year they carefully defined what fishing means, defended fishing as an occupation, and declared that fishing is always to be a primary task of fishermen.

Continually they searched for new and better methods of fishing and for new and better definitions of fishing. Further, they said, "The fishing industry exists by fishing as fire exists by burning." They loved slogans such as "Fishing is the task of every fisherman," "Every fisherman is a fisher," and "A fisherman's outpost for every fisherman's club." They sponsored special meetings called "Fishermen's Campaigns" and "The Month for Fishermen to Fish." They sponsored costly nationwide and worldwide congresses to discuss fishing and to promote fishing and hear about all the ways of fishing such as the new fishing equipment, fish calls, and whether any new bait was discovered.

These fishermen built large, beautiful buildings called "Fishing Headquarters." The plea was that everyone should be a fisherman and every fisher man should fish. One thing they didn't do, however; they didn't fish.

In addition to meeting regularly, they organized a board to send out fishermen to other places where there were many fish. All the fishermen seemed to agree that what is needed is a board that could challenge fishermen to be faithful in fishing. The board was formed by those who had the great vision and courage to speak about fishing, to define fishing, and to promote the idea of fishing in faraway streams and lakes where many other fish of different colors lived.

Also the board hired staffs and appointed committees and held many meetings to define fishing, to defend fishing, and to decide what new streams should be thought about. But the staff and committee members did not fish.

Large, elaborate, and expensive training centers were built whose original and primary purpose was to teach fishermen how to fish. Over the years, courses were offered on the needs of fish, the nature of fish, where to find fish, the psychological reactions of fish, and how to approach and feed fish. Those who taught had doctorates in fishology. But the teachers did not fish. They only taught fishing. Year after year, after tedious training, many were graduated and were given fishing licenses. They were sent to do full-time fishing, some to distant waters that were filled with fish.

Some spent much study and travel to learn the history of fishing and to see faraway places where the founding fathers did great fishing in the centuries past. They lauded the faithful fishermen of years before who handed down the idea of fishing.

Further, the fishermen built large printing houses to publish fishing guides. Presses were kept busy day and night to produce materials solely devoted to fishing methods, equipment, and programs to arrange and to encourage meetings to talk about fishing. A speakers' bureau was also provided to schedule special speakers on the subject of fishing.

Many who felt the call to be fishermen responded. They were commissioned and sent to fish. But like the fishermen back home, they never fished. Like the fishermen back home, they engaged in all kinds of other occupations. They built power plants to pump water for fish and tractors to plow new waterways. They made all kinds of equipment to travel here and there to look at fish hatcheries. Some also said that they wanted to be part of the fishing party, but they felt called to furnish fishing equipment. Others felt that their job was to relate to the fish in a good way so the fish would know the difference between good and bad fishermen. Others felt that simply letting the fish know they were nice, land-loving neighbors and how loving and kind they were was enough.

After one stirring meeting on "The Necessity for Fishing," one young fellow left the meeting and went fishing. The next day he reported that he had caught two outstanding fish. He was honored for his excellent catch and was scheduled to visit all the big meetings possible to tell how he did it. So he quit his fishing in order to have time to tell about the experience to the other fisher men. He was also placed on the Fisher men's General Board as a person having considerable experience.

Now it's true that many of the fisher men sacrificed and put up with all kinds of difficulties. Some lived near the water and bore the smell of dead fish every day. They received the ridicule of some who made fun of their fishermen's clubs and the fact that they claimed to be fishermen yet never fished. They wondered about those who felt it was of little use to attend the weekly meetings to talk about fishing. After all, were they not following the Master, who said, "Follow me, and I will make you fishers of men"?

Imagine how hurt some were when one day a person suggested that those who don't catch fish were really not fishermen, no matter how much they claimed to be. Yet it did sound correct. Is a person a fisherman if year after year he never catches a fish? Is one following if he isn't fishing?

CPSIA information can be obtained
at www.ICGtesting.com
Printed in the USA
BVHW040735130720
583581BV00009B/140